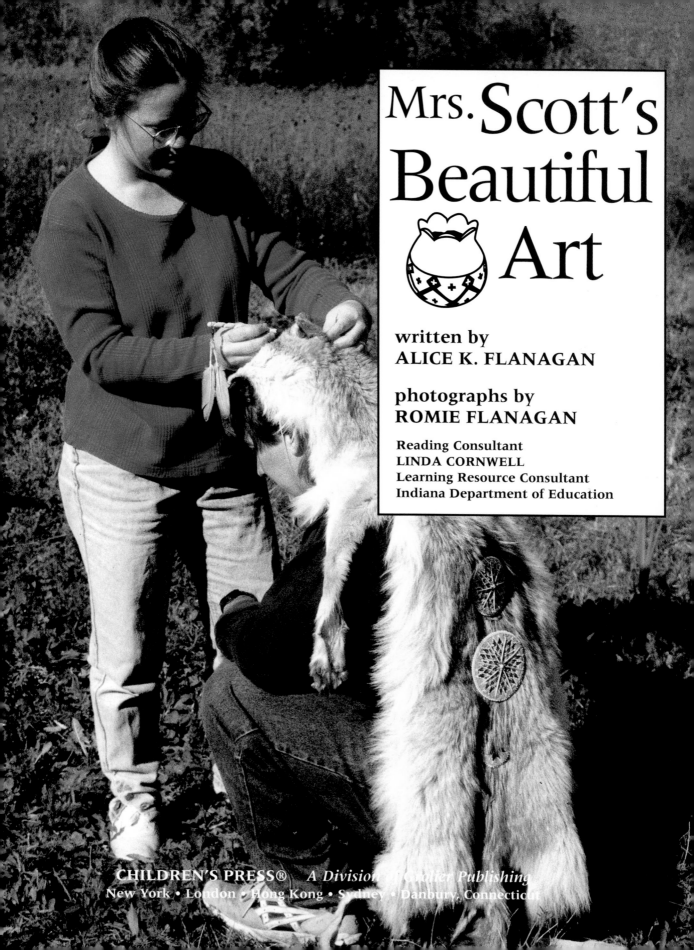

Mrs. Scott's Beautiful Art

written by
ALICE K. FLANAGAN

photographs by
ROMIE FLANAGAN

Reading Consultant
LINDA CORNWELL
Learning Resource Consultant
Indiana Department of Education

CHILDREN'S PRESS® *A Division of Grolier Publishing*
New York • London • Hong Kong • Sydney • Danbury, Connecticut

Special thanks to Robin McBride Scott
for allowing us to tell her story.

Mrs. Scott would like to dedicate this book to her daughter Emeline.
She would like to thank: her husband Mark Scott, her parents Samie
and Phil McBride, her grandparents and all her relatives, Rita Kohn,
Margaret Ann Bird, the Samaniego family, and all the elders who
have taken the time to pass on their knowledge and wisdom.

Visit Children's Press® on the Internet at:
http://publishing.grolier.com

Library of Congress Cataloging-in-Publication Data
Flanagan, Alice K.
   Mrs. Scott's beautiful art / written by Alice K. Flanagan ; photographs
by Romie Flanagan ; reading consultant, Linda Cornwell.
   p. cm. — (Our neighborhood)
   Summary: Describes the activities of a traditional artist who uses
many natural items as she creates art in the tradition of her Cherokee
ancestors.
   ISBN 0-516-21135-8 (lib.bdg.)   0-516-26469-9 (pbk.)
   1. Cherokee art—Juvenile literature. 2. Cherokee Indians—Material
culture—Juvenile literature. 3. Cherokee Indians—Social life and cus-
toms—Juvenile literature. [1. Indian artists. 2. Artists. 3. Occupations.]
I. Flanagan, Romie, ill. II. Title. III. Series: Our neighborhood (New
York, N.Y.)

E99.C5F66 1999
704.03'9755—dc21   98-21498
                                                CIP
                                                AC

Photographs ©: Romie Flanagan

GROLIER
PUBLISHING
1 2 3 4 5 6 7 8 9 10 R 08 07 06 05 04 03 02 01 00 99

Mrs. Scott works quietly in the afternoon sun.

She gathers sweetgrass.

From it she will make a tiny turtle
for a friend.

Mrs. Scott is a traditional artist.
She makes things from plants and
animals the same way her Cherokee
ancestors might have made them a
long time ago.

Mrs. Scott works at home, where she also takes care of her daughter Emeline.

When Mrs. Scott was a little girl,
her grandmother taught her how
to sew with beads.

Other relatives taught her how to sew ribbons on clothing.

Mrs. Scott also went to art school. There, she learned how to paint and how to work with metals.

Mrs. Scott makes many things from plants. From gourds, she makes containers.

12

She teaches others how to paint
and burn pictures on them.

Mrs. Scott buys some of the gourds
she uses. She grows other gourds
from seeds.

14

It takes a long time to scrape out the fruit of the gourd and dry out the shell. Mrs. Scott likes it when Emeline helps her.

Mrs. Scott also makes many things from animals. She made this beautiful headdress for her husband from coyote skin.

16

She made this deerskin dress to wear at her wedding.

Before Mrs. Scott started making the dress, the skin, or hide, looked something like this.

Mrs. Scott scraped off the hair from the hide.

Then she rubbed the hide to make it soft.

Mrs. Scott uses porcupine quills to decorate some of her art. Quills are the sharp spines under a porcupine's hair.

Mrs. Scott heats the quills in water
and makes them different colors.

Mrs. Scott adds a branch from a juniper tree to the water to get a red color.

She heats the quills with the fruit
of a walnut tree to dye them brown.

After the quills dry, Mrs. Scott
flattens them and sews them
on the things she makes.

Mrs. Scott believes that if an animal gives you something, then you have to give it something back. She says, "Whatever I give back I try to make beautiful."

Mrs. Scott never throws away her scraps. She puts scraps of leather outside so a mouse or a bird can build a warm nest with them.

When Mrs. Scott picks plants, she takes only what she will use. She leaves the roots so the plants can still grow.

Before Mrs. Scott begins to work on something she says, "I'm going to make you as beautiful as my hands can make you. When people look at you, they will know how thankful I am for you."

When Mrs. Scott is not working at home, she is teaching others about her art. She is passing on the traditions she learned from her ancestors. Their hands are guiding hers.

Meet the Author
and the Photographer

Alice and Romie Flanagan live in Chicago, Illinois, and have been involved in publishing for many years. Alice is a writer, and Romie is a photographer. As husband and wife, they enjoy working together closely. They hope their books help children learn about the people in their community and how their jobs affect the neighborhood.